Aushim Khetarpal

Publisher:	Aum Sportainment Pvt. Ltd.
39-A, Ground Floor, DDA Flat,
Shahpur Jat, New Delhi - 110049
E-mail : aum.sportainment@gmail.com

People got wooden sticks for dhuni

Baba remembered Shiva before dhuni was lit

CONNECT WITH US

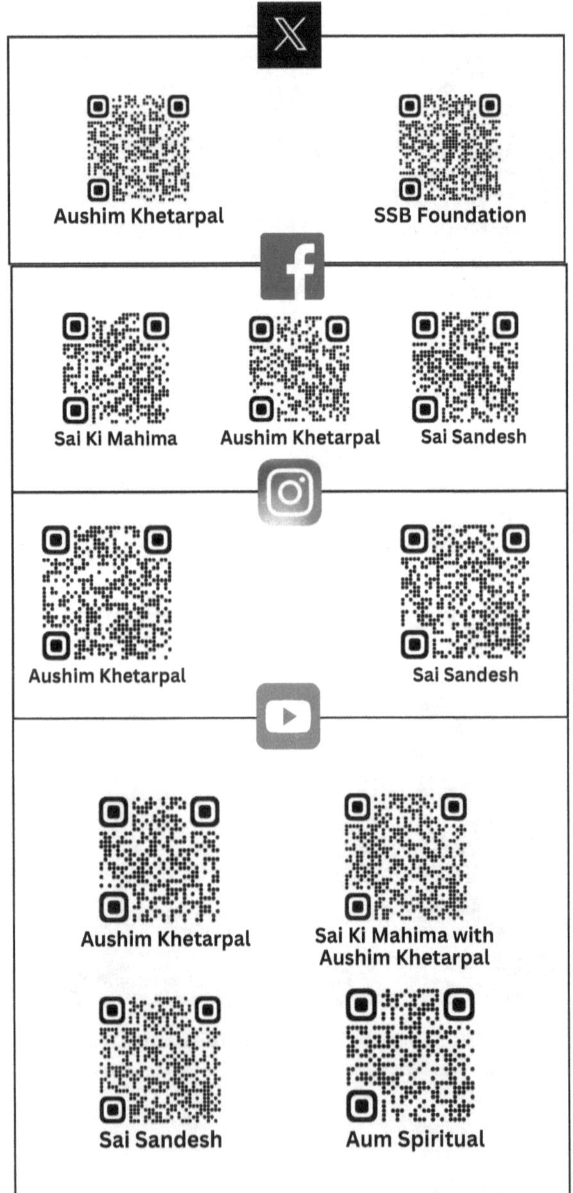

Shirdi Sai Baba Foundation
40-B, First Floor, DDA Flats,
Shahpur Jat, New Delhi-110 049
E-mail: shirdisaibabafoundation@gmail.com

FOREWORD

Vibhuti is a unique and valuable gift of Sadguru Sai. This gift is not only for me or you, but for the whole world. 160 years ago, Sai lit the sacred fire and since then it is burning uninterrupted and Vibhuti born from her womb is still doing welfare to the millions of people every day.

The distinction of Sai's Vibhuti is that it is not just a pinch of ash. Its troubleshooting qualities and preventive utilities are its greatest credibility. 'Vibhuti' not only defeats all three of our physical ailments, but it also gives us a sense of the impermanence of life and also turns us on the path of spirituality.

Sai said, "As long as the world exists, the fire will burn in Dwarkamai and the Dhuni of this fire will keep removing the sufferings from the devotee's life." Just as the ashes of the crematorium became glorified after getting the touch of Lord Shiva, similarly the ash of Dhuni became glorified and got transformed into 'Vibhuti' from the touch of Sai's hands.

When Sai's public welfare Vibhuti came into my hands, I decided to spread the word about Vibhuti's qualities to the world. I collected several facts and started writing a little down about Vibhuti on an ongoing basis. I waited for Sai's blessings to write a book on Vibhuti but Baba did not grant permission immediately. Now that Baba has ordered it, the book is also ready, and in your hands. This echoes the voice of the devotee whose life have benefitted from the Sai Vibhuti.

I am grateful to Sai for granting my dream of making this book on 'Vibhuti' a reality. I am profusely thankful to Dr. Rajinder Kumar Surana (Delhi) for his impeccable editing and for preparing an accurate and pre-planned roadmap for including all facts to be captured in the book. May Sai Baba shower his blessings on Dr. Surana.

Now, I would like to bow in front of Sai baba for blessing me for twenty years and for encouraging me to write this book. I would also like to pay my regards to my father, Late Sh. Purshottam Swarup Khetarpal who always kept Vibhuti in the Puja Ghar and used to bow his head in front of Vibhuti. I also thank my wife, Anita Khetarpal who was fortunate to view Udi emerging from the Photo of Sai Baba at her friend Veena Gupta's house. I also extend my regards to my mother Asha Khetarpal and love for both my daughters, Aarti Khetarpal and Radhika Khetarpal whose love has become my heritage.

||Om Sai Ram I Om Sai Ram ||

Aushim Khetarpal
September 2022

PREVIEW

The author, Aushim ji is mostly aloof and carefree. When it occurs to him, he would concentrate on the grain of mustard, otherwise He would avoid looking at the huge mountain in front of him if did not want to look at it! Why does he do that? The answer is that the writer in him is sensitive to everything around him. It is through the fiber made of his feelings and sensations that he weaves the fabric of creativity. The author can see the presence of the entire Universe even in his small creation.

Aushim Khetarpal did not pick up the super abundance of Sai Nath; rather his micro-vision rested on the little grains of the holy Vibhuti, the remains of Sai Akhand Dhuni (fire).

With a pinch of Vibhuti, he found the divine power and its immeasurable effects. He was mesmerized by the view of the splendor of the Himalayas in a small grain of the Vibhuti. It is the amazing art possessed by Aushim Khetarpal to express even the minutest of feelings so powerfully which is the main reason behind his success.

In the last two decades in the field of Sai literature, around thirty to forty books of Aushim Khetarpal have already been published, which have become very popular. He is always seen dedicatedly worshiping his Supreme Master Sai Baba. His feelings of reverence, faith and compassion have been reflected everywhere in his mind and thinking. This wealth of the author's pure heart and reverence for

Sai Baba has come out beautifully in his new creation 'Sai Vibhuti'.

In the field of Sai literature, 'Sai Vibhuti' is a research work by the author.

Till date, there were no books available exclusively on the supernatural powers of Baba's Vibhuti. This book titled 'Sai Vibhuti' expertly fulfills this void. 'Sai Vibhuti' will definitely create a sense of faith in public life, will bring people closer to Sai and will be helpful in taking care of their physical and spiritual wellbeing. Of course, we are all indebted to the Aushim ji for his unique contribution. With Saikripa and by virtue of his inspiration, Aushim ji should enrich Sai's legacy and inspire lives of all Sai devotees. I wish him best of luck for achievement of all his goals.

Dr. Rajender Kumar Surana,
Ph.D. D. Litt.,
Senior Editor,
International Editors Forum

Date: 21st June, 2021

Table of Contents

VIBHUTI KI MAA: DHOONI MAA

Sai's Dhuni

About 160 years ago, a young fakir came to Shirdi village in Kopargaon taluka of Ahmednagar district of Maharashtra. There, he camped in the broken, deserted mosque of Shirdi Village. He collected firewood from around the area and lit the Fire (Dhuni) with his hands. This Dhuni is still eternal and is kept constantly ignited and is the source of the sacred Vibhuti. The word Dhuni literally means, 'constant, uninterrupted, unbroken and eternal fire. Sai's Dhuni is adorned with these qualities. The word Dhuni is composed of melodies. The word Dhun (Tune) literally means melodious voice or sound. In fact, when Dhuni burns, a moderate sound of ignition continues to emerge. Dhuni says that if you worship and circumambulate this Panchabhuta created by God, the compassionate cry within you will be removed and the moderate waves of happiness in life will begin to sound.

The flame of this Dhuni will always burn

The young fakir must have promised to God that, "the flame of this smoke will burn forever." The young fakir would roam the forests of the village and pick wood. With those sticks, he kept the Dhuni alive every day. After a few years, there was a major disruption; in Shirdi and its adjoining areas, there was a severe outbreak of cholera epidemic. People had to stay in homes. The gram panchayat stopped allowing meeting of people, similar to the COVID-19 lockdown. The movement of goods

coming from the neighboring areas also stopped. The streets were deserted and normal life came to a standstill. People were forced to obey the orders of the village head, Panch and Sarpanch.

Sai had two important questions before Him. Either he should leave the mosque every day to arrange wood for Dhunimai's food to protect Him, but this would mean ignoring the gram panchayat's order every day. Or the second option was to buy a fully loaded wooden cart from another village so that Dhunimai's would have an uninterrupted supply for a month or two, but that would also have violated the gram panchayat's order. The key question before Sai was how to arrange wood. He found the answer to His question within His soul and He was also able to solve His problem by Himself. From another village, Sai bought a cart of wood. He brought the cart to the border of Shirdi. The cart reached the entrance of the mosque and the logs were stocked up in the mosque. Sai used to give more importance to Dhunimai rather than any other individual. To protect Dhunimai, Sai did not accept the order of gram panchayat. He was guided by His intuition.

Incineration bath (BhasmSnan)

While Sai used to sit in the mosque, his devotees also sat near Him. Always, there was smoke spreading all over and on the sides. Smoke from the Dhuni and flying soot also used to fall on the devotees. Every devotee sitting in front of Sai used to bathe in ashes with utmost concentration and devotion. Those moments of bathing in soot had special significance in the life of all His devotees.

Dhuni Pujan

Then and now during the period of Saibaba, the size of the Dhuni used to be 7-feet long and 5.2-feet wide. Devotees used to offer pieces of wood, Uplay (Cow's dung), navdhan, ghee, panch-pavitra wood with their hands. It is no longer possible to do so. Shirdi Sansthan has put iron nets around it.

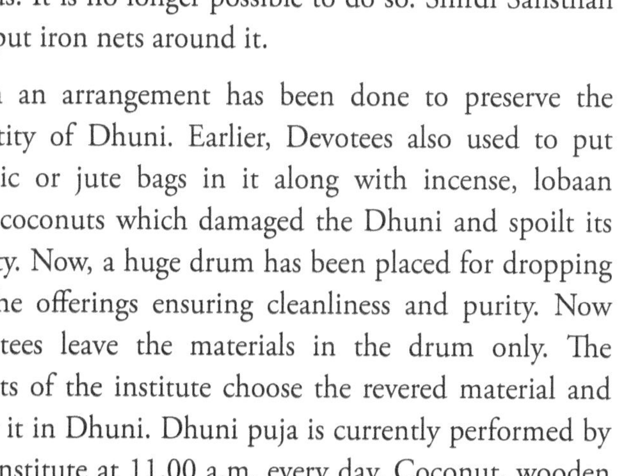

Such an arrangement has been done to preserve the sanctity of Dhuni. Earlier, Devotees also used to put plastic or jute bags in it along with incense, lobaan and coconuts which damaged the Dhuni and spoilt its purity. Now, a huge drum has been placed for dropping all the offerings ensuring cleanliness and purity. Now devotees leave the materials in the drum only. The priests of the institute choose the revered material and offer it in Dhuni. Dhuni puja is currently performed by the institute at 11.00 a.m. every day. Coconut, wooden pieces, dry shells, ghee etc. are placed in the Dhuni. The priests of the Samadhi temple worship the fire of Dhuni (Vaishva-Deva) and give food-ahuti (ghee mixed with cooked rice).

During Sai Baba's existence, this work was often done at Sai's command and performed by Sagun Meru Nayak.

The Spiritual Benefits of Dhuni Fire

There is a spiritual significance behind offering food to the fire of dhuni (Vaishvadeva). therein day-to-day life, we walk around for several purposes, work, shopping, visiting friends and family, etc. In this process of walking on roads and pavements, various insects, small animals,

flies and mosquitoes die under our feet. This leads to having committed grave sin. To get rid of the karma of this unintended sin, Sai instructed devotees to feed sugar or flour to ants or feed bread or grains to dogs, cows and birds. If this is not possible, Sai ordered to offer food in Dhuni to get rid of such sins. The food offered in Dhuni or Vaishvadeva liberates us from the sins of this day-to-day violence against innocent living beings.

Every work of Sai was full of conscience, wisdom, knowledge and spirituality. Every now and then in Sai's works and words, we get a glimpse of philosophy, love for nature, virtue, good deeds, fair policies, guiding principles, yoga, devotion, spirituality and righteousness. Sai's biography is a vast repository of education and teaching. It is up to us how much we understand his teachings and how many of these noble teachings we try to implement into our lives.

The Supernatural Importance of Dhuni

Sai has also explained to us the way to attain Parbrahmeshwar through the medium of burning Dhuni.

Every human being in the world suffers from greed, anger, ego, illusion and jealousy. In the life of a man, six enemies do mean things to spoil his life. A man should avoid bad thoughts, lust, theft, snobbery, false harassment, adultery, and other sinful activities. The fire of all these disorders keeps on burning within us at all times. In this burning fire, our power to work and achieve good results (karmaja Shakti), good deeds, virtues, devotion for following teachings of our religions - these get destroyed. This fire destroys us both ways, from inside and outside us. It is the fire of our worldly life and it is the fire of our materialism. This fire is the result of our desire for possession of more and more worldly things.

Sai instructs us not to nourish wants and desires. He directs us to dump every thought and action for such goals into the fire of Dhuni. He also tells us to throw our false pride in the fire of Dhuni. By doing this, we will become innocent, pure and full of devotion. It is the pure soul of a man that attracts God in his soul. Sai's Dhuni asks us to throw our vices into its fire and pave the way for the attainment of Liberation (Moksha).

Dhuni is like a Yagna

Offering food to Dhuni is like offering desires to burn in Dhuni. This is confirmed through these verses of the Gita.

Lord Krishna says: The spiritually-minded, who eat food that is first offered in sacrifice, are released from all kinds of sin. Others, who cook food for their own enjoyment, verily eat only sin.

Food allows people to live. Food is produced from rain. Rain arises from sacrifice. Actions produce sacrifice or Yagna.

God produces knowledge. Knowledge produces actions. Actions produce sacrifice or yagya.

Where there is sacrifice, the omnipresent God is also there.

It is clear that when a person is able to devote all food items to the fire of the world or the Sun God, he always remains protected from bad effects of all types

of sins. Whenever you devote food, you must also offer archana, pujan, Vandana and kirtan. to vaishvadeva. It is this righteous conduct that frees you from your sins. Sai instructs us to always place food or other qualified materials in Dhuni with full devotion. Sai Baba, with mercy on the masses, lit Dhuni for our benefit and also advised us for pujan of Dhuni.

If Dhuni is so glorious, how glorified will the Vibhuti arising out of Dhuni's womb be!

VIBHUTI

Sai's Vibhuti

'Vibhuti' is a precious substance produced from the womb of the Dhuni mother. 'Vibhuti' means treasure, precious wealth, gems, ashes. In the Scriptures, the remains obtained as a result of burning of any materials such as cow dung, wood etc. are called ash (Vibhuti). The fire that Sai lit with his hands burns continuously and he collected ashes or Udi as a Master. Even today, a large number of Vibhutis are distributed to devotees who use them for healing physically and from within as well

Need for Vibhuti

Sai used to have many patients visiting him for relief from various diseases. Many of them were suffering from incurable diseases. Baba was not a doctor, a Vaidya or a Surgeon. To cure devotees, he didn't feel anyone's pulse, didn't perform any type of test and didn't write any prescription of medicine. He was just an easy going fakir. He had his own ways of preventing and curing diseases. Once, a man's eyes were swollen; Sai grinded the bibel seed and placed it on his eyes. The next day, that man's eyes got completely healed. One person named Butti was suffering from diarrhea disease. Sai asked him to eat pistachios and almonds and drink milk and his diarrhea stopped. Sai used to treat people in his bizarre ways and always cured people satisfactorily. When more and more people started visiting after hearing about Baba's healing powers, Sai adopted another method. Now he started applying Vibhuti on the affected body part of the

person suffering from the disease. Some were fed with Vibhuti mixed in water. The patient's disease used to go away slowly and thus Sai gave huge relief to his devotees. Sai also gave Vibhuti for the prevention of the diseases as well. Sai did this throughout his life. Such was the power of Sai's touch. I was an atheist. Studying medicine was beyond me. He first pulled me towards him, purified me and then started telling bhakts to listen to my weird answers and solutions. / am like a hanuman who only knows to chant Sai's name and know that my faith in Sai will heal his bhakts as their faith in me is being blessed by my faith in him. They would all get cured by my weird answer. But when I analysed, HIS medicines were correct. It had logic. I used to wonder why me. The answer is the master wants surrender and put faith in him. He doesn't want you to question. He then gives you his powers. For every master wants his pupil to touch the sky.

Tilak of Blessings

Sai Vibhuti was also used in another form. When someone was travelling from Shirdi, Sai would place a long tilak of Vibhuti on his forehead and then allowed him to leave Shirdi. For using on the way, Sai would also give them a handful of Udi. If Sai wished for his devotee to stay, Sai wouldn't apply a Tilak on his forehead; it was indication that Sai was stopping them for some reason. Sai was a trikalgyata - a person with the power of knowing about past, present and future of the Universe. Sai had knowledge of the future events about to happen in the lives of His devotees. If Baba sensed that there could be difficulties on the way, or if there was a bad day ahead, Sai would not allow the person to proceed or even contemplate his departure from Shirdi. Those who received Udi from Baba at the time of their departure, always felt that Baba had given an auspicious blessing to them and was protecting them.

Mythological Significance of Vibhuti

Vibhuti also has mythological significance. Lord Shiv used to apply Bhasma (Vibhuti) on his whole body every day. He always kept his body wrapped in Vibhuti. No other god in Hindu mythology has ever been seen covered with an ash coat on his body. Hanuman ji used to apply oil mixed with vermilion on his body; but he did not consume it. Bhasma (Vibhuti) must be having some special significance, that is why Lord Shiva used to apply it on his body. Generally people considered Bhasma as useless remains from burning of anything; but Lord Shiva glorified it by applying it on His body. Sai knew the importance of Bhasm; He also glorified Vibhuti with the touch of His hands.

Spiritual Benefits of Vibhuti

Sai Baba has made us all aware of the spiritual importance of Vibhuti. Sai explains it through a beautiful metaphor. He says this universe is like an eternal burning furnace. A man's life is like a piece of wood burning in a furnace. The ash obtained after the burning of wood is a reflection of the working of the universe. At the end, the ultimate result of all human lives and other living beings is reduced to a handful of Ash, or dust. This is the eternal truth of our lives. Any being including humans that are made of Panchabhuta (Five elements) comes into the universe by virtue of Birth. After leaving his mortal body,

i.e. when he dies, the Panchabhuta get absorbed back into 'Panchabhuta' - the source of everything; and what is left behind is just a handful of ash that is saved as a relic. Sai Bhasma (Vibhuti) signifies the mortality of life. Sai also reveals that the root-conscious of this universe is all mortal, even the whole world is mortal. What is immortal is only God. God has been present since time immemorial, is present now, and will always be there in the future. God will remain forever as He is timeless. In this world, we live among our families, relationships, friends, wealth, glory and all other material pursuits. It's all short-lived and perishable. The creature comes into this world empty handed and leaves from here empty handed. The Vibhuti instills this sense of mortality in the conscience of the human and make him humbler and kind towards others.

Sai's Udi expresses the nirveda bhaav. Eternal Peace in our lives. It gives us the message of renunciation and dispassion. Renunciation and Dispassion - these are two emotions that make our mind free, reduce attachment and help us to cross the cosmic ocean of being. Sai urges us to look at the ashes well with eyes open wide. This beautiful body of yours will one day be converted into the same ashes. You have received human life as the blessing of God and as His very special and precious gift. You have worn the chola of man because of many accumulated virtuous deeds done by you in previous births. Before this chola is converted back into ashes, you should do good deeds, adopt righteousness, remember God, devote your life for others and your Dharma, try to achieve the ultimate goal of your life. What is the

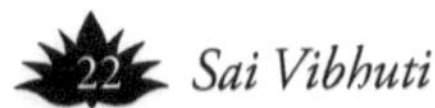

guarantee in life? No one knows when Life will cheat on you. No one knows when suddenly vital life will be snatched away! It is this uncertainty of Life that makes you feel as a mortal person. Sai says that before the evening of life suddenly appears before your eyes and the body is reduced to ashes, you should choose and follow the lessons of knowledge, devotion, good deeds and yoga. Gear up to walk on it, be sure to get into practice and fulfill the purpose of life. Those who do not do this even while wearing the priceless chola of human body, they hurt themselves! They never reach to a peaceful fate as they keep on wandering aimlessly in different forms in this world in search of eternity. Look at the image of the universe and decide in advance what path you should follow.

Ramte Ram Aao Ji, Udia Ki Gonia Lao Ji

Shirdi's women used to gather and go to Sai and sing this song on the way- "Ramte Ram Aao ji, Udia Ki Gonia Laoji." Even while sitting in front of Sai they used to sing the same song. Through this song, they prayed to Sai, "O Ram, O my God, O my Sai, may you be happy and bless Udi." Sai used to give them a handful of Udi on their way back home. Sai also sang this song when he was overwhelmed. This shows us how important Sai's Udi was for everyone at Shirdi.

Devotees pay homage to Udi

There are feelings of faith and reverence in the minds of people towards Udi or Vibhuti. During Sai's presence, devotees used to bow their heads and accept it with both hands whenever they received Udi from Sai. Udi was

kept wrapped in paper or a piece of cloth. After coming to his house, the devotees used to keep Udi in the place of worship. Many people thought it to be worthy of worship and applied on their foreheads regularly. Many people used to drink it regularly after mixing in water, whether they felt comfortable or sick. Even today, millions of devotees come to Shirdi every day. After darshan, they are also given Udi along with prasad on behalf of the Sansthan. Devotees reverentially accept it by bowing and touching it with the head. On reaching back, they keep Udi safe in their puja room or in the temple. Udi always removes the sufferings of devotees who have faith and reverence in the power of Udi. Udi is an herb for remedy to cure a hundred diseases.

Udi is like the precious Chintamani Gemstone

A single cure for a hundred diseases

With the blessings of Sai, Vibhuti has unmatched qualities to completely cure a variety of diseases and give relief from suffering. So m any devotees have experienced its amazing benefits. Many people got rid of mental illnesses and many others observed the special miracles of Udi. Some miraculous experiences of devotees with the use of Udi have been highlighted in the later sections. In fact, after having seen and heard about so many magical experiences, there is no doubt to claim that the Vibhuti, has proved to be a single cure for so many different types of diseases.

Cure from Tuberculosis

A doctor used to live in Malegaon in the Nashik district of Maharashtra. His nephew was suffering with tuberculosis

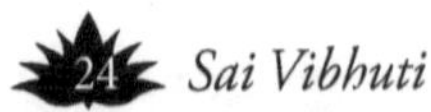

In fact, tuberculosis at the time of Sai, was incurable. The doctor got his nephew to undergo all types of medical treatments, but there was no respite and the disease continued to advance. Once a friend of the doctor who was a Sai devotee advised, "Take him to Shirdi. He will surely get cured with the blessings of Sai."

The boy's parents brought the child to Shirdi. Feeling clueless and very sad, the parents prayed to Sai, "O Sai Nath! We have been disappointed in every way as our child is suffering and we are not able to find any cure. Now, we have come to your shelter as we know that you are a troubleshooter and only you can cure him. Have pity on this child, we have full faith in you." Sai asked the child to apply Udi on his body. Then Baba told to his parents, "The one who climbs the stairs of this mosque, all his troubles get removed. You must have faith in God. This child will be completely cured in a week's time. This mosque is Dwarkamai. Baba applied Udi on the body of the child with His hands. Within seven days, the child recovered from tuberculosis and became fully healthy.

Cancer goes away

Dr. Pillay's cancer disease was also healed by the Vibhuti. Dr. Pillay was an ardent devotee of Sai. He was suffering from cancer disease. A lot of treatment was done but there was no cure. He suffered from severe and intolerable pain. Dr. Pillay could see his end nearing him anytime. He told Dixit, "The pain of cancer is becoming unbearable. It is better to die instead of suffering with so much pain. Please ask Baba to grant me death so that I get some relief from this torture. For my remaining karma - I will

bear its consequences in my next lives." Dixit relayed the message to Sai. Baba said, "Doctor need not panic. He will not need to suffer till his next life; his bad karma will be finished in ten days. He should not worry about death at all. Kaka! Bring please bring him here right now by lifting him on your back."

Around four or five people lifted Dr. Pillay and brought him in front of Baba. Baba laid him down on the bed near Him and placed a pillow under the head of Dr. Pillay. The bandage that was tied on the wound was quickly removed. Baba comforted Dr. Pillai saying, "right now a black crow will come here. He will strike with his beak on your wound and then you will be healed." It was evening and it had become a bit dark inside the mosque. Abdul, a sweeper, came to clean the area inside the mosque. Due to darkness, he could not see and accidently his foot touched the cancer wound of Dr. Pillay. The wound ruptured and seven poisonous insects came out of it. Dr. Pillay started moaning in severe pain. He couldn't understand what was happening!

Suddenly a crow named Abdul appeared from nowhere and struck with its beak on the wound of Dr. Pillay and flew away. Later, Sai cleansed the wound and applied Udi on it. After ten days, the wound dried up completely. With the blessings of Sai, the Udi destroyed the cancer and Dr. Pillay was completely cured.

The lumps disappeared

Shama's younger brother used to live in a village called Savli Viheer near Shirdi. His wife got diagnosed with plague and due to this, big lumps appeared all over her body. Shama's younger brother reached Shirdi at night. He told Shama the whole situation and asked him to go and ask for Baba's help. Shama went to meet Baba and requested for urgent help for his brother's wife. He also asked Baba for permission to go home.

Sai told Shama, "Take this Udi and send it to your younger brother's home. Allah will definitely heal his wife. Why do you want to go back at night? You can go in the morning and return on the same day itself."

Shama's younger brother reached back home with the blessed Udi. He mixed the holy Udi in water and gave it to his wife to drink. Within few minutes, first she experienced high sweating and after that the fever subsided. Lumps from her body also disappeared.

The problem of fainting cured

There used to be an Iranian monsieur family in Mumbai. –Every two to four hours, his daughter would repeatedly faint, and her hands and feet got stiffened. Sometimes she fainted and fell to the ground. The Iranian gentleman consulted the best doctors for her treatment but to no avail. Once, some of his friends advised him to take the girl to Shirdi. If they could arrange to get Udi from any of Sai devotees, he can mix the Udi in water and give it to the girl. It may help the girl child to heal soon. Kaka Saheb Dixit lived close to the Iranian master's house. The Iranian monsieur visited him and explained about his girl's health issues. Dixit gave him a small pack of Vibhuti and asked to mix the Udi in water daily and ask his daughter to drink it with faith in Sai Baba. The Iranian monsieur did the same. In a few days, his daughter got

completely cured, became healthy and she never fainted again. Such is the effect of Sai's Vibhuti!

Unencumbered delivery

Ramgir Buva was making spiritual progress in the company of Sai. One day he came to Baba and said "Deva! Give me permission. I want to go to my house." Baba said "You can go. But please do one of my works. While going, visit Jamnagar from Jalgaon on the way. Go and meet Nana Sahib. Give him my blessings. From there your house is near, then you can go to your house." After saying this, Baba gave him one packet of Udi and also gave him 'Aarti Sai Baba' created by Adkar.

Ramgir told Sai with a bit of hesitation "Baba! I have only two rupees with me. I am worried of how will I be able to travel further?" Sai said, "All your worries will be taken care of. You must leave soon." Ramgir reached Jalgaon at three o'clock in the night. Only two Annas were left in his pocket. Now, he wondered how he could reach Jamnagar? Meanwhile, a man reached there looking for Ramgir Buva. He told Ramgir that Nana Saheb had sent a Tonga to receive him and to reach Nana Saheb's house. Ramgir accompanied the Tonga driver to Nana Saheb's place. The Tonga stopped in front of Nana Saheb's office in the morning. Ramgir got down and went to relieve himself. When he came back there was neither the Tonga nor its driver! After enquiring about from many people, he finally reached Nana's home and entered the courtyard.

Nana Saheb's daughter was moaning with labour pain as she was about to give birth to a child. Nana Saheb was praying for his daughter's well-being in front of Sai's

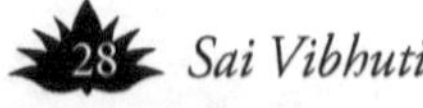

picture. Ramgir handed over the packet of Udi and Aarti sent by Baba for Nana Saheb. Nana Saheb had tears of joy in his eyes on receiving Udi from Baba. He immediately added Udi to the water and fed it to his daughter. Then they started singing Aarti praising Sai Baba. Within few minutes, the pain subsided and Nana Saheb's daughter felt better and she was able to go through the process of delivery without any problem. Such is the glory of Sai.

End of nightmares

A person named Kayastha Prabhu lived in the Bandra area of Mumbai. He was suffering from insomnia for many days. Whenever he slept at night, he had shocking dream of his late father as if he was standing in front of him and yelling and showering abuses on him. This led to insomnia and restlessness. He could not sleep throughout the nights. He went to consult many doctors but the treatment was not successful. One day his friend gave him a suggestion. "Please take a packet of Sai Vibhuti and put it under your pillow."

Kayastha Prabhu did that and went off to sleep very well. For a month he did not get any dream. Prabhu started praying to Sai every Thursday and his packet of Vibhuti under his pillow; he was never again troubled him with insomnia.

Balaji's Wife

Once Balaji's wife was making arrangement to celebrate their marriage anniversary. They had invited relatives, friends and the people of the village. Unexpectedly, more than three times people came to attend the program whereas the food was not arranged for such

a large gathering. Balaji's wife got scared after seeing this situation. Balaji was worried that how would they be able to serve so many people and what kind of food will everyone be able to get? If the arrangement was not done immediately, more than half of the people might have to go back without having food. Immediately a thought arose in his mind. He called the daughter-in-law and asked her to bring Sai's Udi that was kept in the Pujagriha. He told her to put small quantity of Udi in each vessel of the food and cover each vessel with clean cloth. Then, he told her to offer food to Baba at first and only after that distribute the rest of the food among guests. "Baba will surely take care that nobody points a finger on us due to any reason. This is the food from Sai's home, then how can anyone go hungry from here without eating Sai's prasad?"

The daughter-in-law did exactly the same. Eventually, with grace of Baba, all the guests were able to enjoy the food. The daughter-in-law looked into the pots and was surprised to find that there was still a lot of food left in the vessels. This is the wonder of Sai's blessing. Sai's Vibhuti is the treasure of Sai and the treasure of God never decreases. In fact, many such stories and incidents have happened during Sai's life, where people have vouched for the miraculous effects of Udi in their lives.

Me and Vibhuti

It was the auspicious day of 27th July 1997. I reached Shirdi with my wife and children. This was my first visit to Shirdi. On reaching Shirdi, I first came in front of Dhunimai. The rich fire burning from the hands of Sai

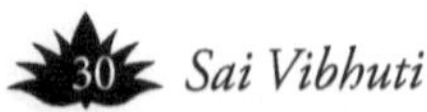

was burning relentlessly. I stood in front of the fire of Dhunimai. My family members were behind me.

We started meditating for a while. Suddenly, I felt as if a bright light was slowly entering into my closed eyes. In pure white light, I saw a fakir, with a white beard, wearing a long Shirt (kafni). Suddenly. after a few moments, the appearance of Vittal (Shri Krishna) standing on the brick was felt. After this, there was a feeling of presence of Lord Shiva who was seen sitting on the rocks at Mount Kailash. After some time, I could see right in front of me Jesus Christ hanging on the cross, with raised hands as if forgiving everyone for their sins! Again in the next moment, I could read the text of Holy books of the Gita and *Quransharif* moving in front of my eyes. After some time, I could feel the presence of a fakir with a long white beard, wearing a white Kafni, standing just near me. I was totally confused and was not able to understand what was happening and why it was happening with me!

While I was wondering about all this visions, I could hear a voice whispering in my ears "So, after all, you have come to me dear Arjun. I have been waiting for a long time. You are a true person. I am the one whom you have come here to meet. See! This is my real form."

Hesitatingly I replied, "But I am an atheist. I don't have any belief in any deity till today." The voice of the fakir again echoed in the ears. "Some people are obsessed with God, whereas some people become atheist. Ultimately, sooner or later, all atheists come to realize that God indeed exists and thereafter, their life changes completely, Arjun! Now since you have come to me, let me apply this

paste of reverence on you." Suddenly, I felt as if someone was touching my forehead with the thumb of his hand, applying mark on it.

After a few moments, the voice of the fakir again echoed in the ears. "Remember, the soul is always traveling in the Universe. It keeps on coming repeatedly into this world. I have been watching the journey of the soul since time immemorial. I meet all souls in each re-birth. I give them guidance and bring them on the way to truth and devotion. That is my karma. You must tell the people of the world about me. *You have to spread my words among the masses so that their lives change for the good. This task is very difficult, but I will remove all difficulties towards attainment of your goals.* Take this Vibhuti and keep on applying it daily, and all your problems will get solved. This Vibhuti is going to play an important role in your life." It was only after around two hours that I regained consciousness. My whole body was sweating. I saw in front of me a thick mesh of iron around Dhunimai and Sai Vibhuti was coming out near the net in front of me. I recalled how my father used to keep Vibhuti in his room of worship. There must be a very special significance of Vibhuti. I applied Vibhuti on my forehead, and also on the forehead of my family members. Then I picked up little quantity of Vibhuti from Dhunimai, rolled it up in a piece of paper and safely put it in my pocket. I got up in front of Dhunimai, bowed my head and proceeded towards the next place. I had absolutely no clue where was I going? There was an invisible force that was holding and guiding me from one place to another. I got in the queue as I walked with the crowd towards Sai Temple.

 Sai Vibhuti

After about one and a half hours later I was bowing in front of Sai's Samadhi.

I was very much surprised when I looked at the face of Sai baba's statue. It resembled exactly with the face of the Fakir whom I had seen sitting in front of Dhoonimai! From those moments, I started realizing and believing in the existence of the huge powers of Sai Baba.

After visiting the Samadhi temple, I reached under a neem tree where people were moving around (called as doing 'Pradakshina') the tree and bowing their head in one place. I came to know that it was the same neem tree under which the young fakir used to sit for hours and hours and due to his divine influence, the fruit and leaves of Neem became sweetened. I also did pradakshina and sat under the neem tree. After a while, I was sitting in the posture of meditation. Slowly again, a bright supernatural light started coming in front of my closed eyes. In this divine light, the picture of the fakir wearing a white Kafni emerged again. The fakir said, "Listen to me carefully. Read about my magical powers. Try to understand my cosmic and supernatural works. You will find that I am always ready to help my devotees. Listen to the music of the divine, the ultimate power in your soul. It is always echoing. Just listen to it and try to understand it. This music is playing day and night, in each moment of your life. I am playing this music. Whenever this music enters your ears, it will dissolve the nectar in your heart and you will start feeling divinity in yourself."

My eyes were closed. In meditation I was feeling the direct access to the fakir in Sai. Both my hands folded in front of the divine statue and I said, "Oh my Sai Baba! I was an atheist, a fool. I never tried to come at your door. Definitely, it is your power that has drawn me here and I am in front of you today. I had to go somewhere to find solace. What else could I do? All the doors were closed for me in this world. Whatever wealth and abundance came in the flow of time, it was blown away just like a pile of sand.

Friends and other people known to me broke away from me, relatives abandoned me. Such circumstances wreaked havoc, a cloud of crisis broke and I was treated as inferior to others and was left empty-handed. Earlier I used to be filled with false ego, and within no time the ego melted like snow.

Today I am nothing but a stone lying on the road. Baba, still you called me at your place to bless me. This is your greatness. Truly you are the Father of Orphans."

Sai's image was in front of me. The fakir laid his hand on my head and said, "Listen to me, my Son! Money and splendor are worldly things. These might be available to you today, but may not be there tomorrow. Till yesterday, when you had all these things, you were egoistic and an atheist. It is good that money and splendor are all gone now. Just see, there is no more ego. Now you are obsessed with divinity. You may not have understood that till yesterday. You were in deep sleep. Today you have awakened by renouncing sleep. You must think yourself fortunate. Your sleeping luck has also awakened now. Now that you have woken up, do not be tempted to go back to sleep. Awakening is life, remaining in deep slumber is death. Now I want to give you something that I give to only a few chosen ones. That object is spiritual knowledge. You are getting it from me to keep sharing with the world. It is such wealth that grows more by distributing to others. Today the world is suffering. Try to make the unhappy world happy. Today, there are millions of people in the world who are living in worse condition than yours. Always look at them with compassion and love. Today most people in the world do not know about devotion to God. Tell them about me."

I folded my hands to the divine power and said, "O statue of compassion, you are the father of the devotees, you are the mother of the devotees, you are also the brother and friend of the devotees. You accepted me as your son. The world had rejected me, but you hugged me!

I am blessed. I do not know which magic mantra you have recited for me, that an atheist has become a devotee forever. After having you in my life, I feel blessed that I have received the biggest diamond of compassion from this universe Baba. In you, I have found the powers of the divine God. Now, whatever command you give me to perform, I will do it."

The voice of the fakir reverberated in my ears, "O my son! Only when you destroy your ego completely, will I accept you in my refuge. In future, you must not fall into the turmoil of the world, just stay away from them. You will do all my work, only mine, and nobody else's. You have to spread my life's lessons and the glory from

house to house. Now all you have to do is to burn the light of devotion in the hearts of people. You just have to spread my words of compassion and empathy amongst people. Let me tell you this, that from today, you will present the story of my life to the people, write holy text, distribute my Vibhuti with your own hands to the needy people, for the purpose of public welfare; and you will also construct my Dham (place of worship) in Vrindavan. This is my blessing to you. You may not know that I have specially chosen you to do something extraordinary on this earth. I will guide you by remaining in the backstage and will keep on infusing power in you to complete your life's missions. Just like Lord Krishna, I will control the direction of your life's chariot so that you don't lose the sight of your goals. You must realize that I am pulling you away from worldly desires. I have hardened your mind so that you become firm and focused on your life's mission. Now you will experience complete freedom from the bindings of the world, even while living in this world. No relationships, no friends or anything in the society will be able to control your activities. You will move around like a gust of fresh air. I firmly believe that you will be able to heal the wounds of the people in this unhappy world and consider their sorrow as your sorrow. My hand of blessings will always be on your head."

Pointing his finger towards an unknown direction, Baba further told me, "Son, you must follow the path of truth. You will never face any obstacle anywhere. No matter how many problems you have to face, do not follow the wrong path in your life, ever."

"I have given you the power of managing your insight and the internal power to face anything in your life with strength. Your every task will be completed successfully. You are going to make all my wishes come true."

After that, Baba applied Vibhuti with holy powers on my forehead and became invisible. By applying holy Vibhuti, I felt as if Baba had endorsed my internal powers to work for completion of His missions. I opened my eyes. Sai's divine form was still lighting its aura in front of my eyes like bright lights. After some time when I regained my composure–, a few leaves fell from the neem tree and landed on my lap. An atheist had become a believer. Considering the neem leaves as Sai Vibhuti, I bowed my head in front of them, and ate them with reverence.

I returned back from Shirdi. For a period of two and a half years, I did not put Vibhuti on the forehead, rather used to consume small portions. After some time, I started applying Vibhuti on my neck. I believe that one must not publicly display performing any task; rather it should be done discreetly. Therefore, even applying Vibhuti on the neck is an expression of one's our reverence for Sai.

In order to complete the projects of Sai Baba, Shirdi Sai Baba Foundation Trust was established to work on a large scale and to give realization to the words given by Him. Presently more than three million people are associated with Shirdi Sai Baba Foundation. There are around two and a half million people who pay respects to Vibhuti everyday by placing it on their tongue and consuming it. Sadhguru Sai has immense blessings on all his devotees. The corona virus has spread fiercely in

the world for almost one year. We salute those people who consume Sai's Udi daily, those who believe in the holy powers of Sai and chant His name and perform Puja regularly. It is a pleasant surprise that all the people associated with Shirdi Sai Baba Foundation are still protected by the grace of Sai Baba and no one has been affected by this dreaded Corona virus. I consider myself very fortunate that Sai Baba blessed me and gave me an opportunity in which I continue to provide Sai's Udi to all the members of the Trust. As the Chief Trustee of Shirdi Sai Baba Foundation, it was also my ultimate duty and responsibility to take care of all members and to protect them by distributing Baba's Udi amongst them.

Here, I have an important information to share with all readers. We are establishing Saidham in Vrindavan.

Since 20th April 2020, Sai Baba's uninterrupted Dhooni is burning brightly at Saidham. Holy Vibhuti for devotees is also being provided there. In case of any query with regard to Vibhuti, kindly visit the Website of Shirdi Sai Baba Foundation www. ssbf.co.in and send your details.

VIBHUTI'S MAGIC IS FOREVER

A film on Baba has been completed

It was the January of 2000. There was a program at my house which was attended by film director Deepak Balraj. At that time the issue of Kargil war was a hot topic in the country. All two of us were discussing about making a film on Kargil war. The script writing work on the story was also almost complete.

There was a big picture of Baba that adorned the wall in the room where we were sitting. Suddenly I noticed something strange happening on the picture of Baba. For a moment I could not believe my eyes. Baba's Vibhuti was coming out of Baba's photo. I immediately got up and applied a pinch of Vibhuti on my forehead. Vibhuti coming out of the picture was amazing and intriguing. Deepak Balraj also witnessed this amazing incident.

Suddenly a thought flashed in Deepak's mind, "Why don't we make a film on Baba? Baba has many supernatural powers. There are millions of people who have experienced amazing effects of Sai Baba's supernatural powers! If a film is made on Sai, then people will get truthful information about Sai. Let us cancel the idea of a film on Kargil war. Instead, we will make a film on Sai Baba." My thoughts had changed as soon as I applied Vibhuti from the photo on my forehead.

Deepak then told Vikas Kapoor, "Now please start writing the script on Sai Baba." Vikas Kapoor expressed

his inability and said, "Sorry friend, I will not be able to write script for Sai Baba film."

The next day, at around 6 A.M., Deepak's wife received a call from Vikas Kapoor. He excitedly told Deepak's wife Kishori that he saw Sai Baba in his dream, and Baba was beating Vikas with a Satka (wooden stick) because Vikas was sleeping; and Baba wanted him to wake up immediately. This dream made Vikas understand the meaning of the dream as an indicator to Baba's will. Now, Vikas was feeling motivated and was ready to write the script for the film to be made on Sai Baba's life.

Finally, the work on the film commenced in January 2000. Had the Vibhuti not come out of the picture, then how could we have understood the wish of Baba? Vibhuti changed our mind set and finally, we all started the project with reverence and love for our Sai. During the shooting of the film, everyone used to first apply Vibhuti on their forehead to receive blessings of Sai, and then started the work on shooting. The film was released on 6 September 2001 throughout the world. With the blessings of Sai Baba, the film was a huge box office success. Everyone enjoyed the film. With blessings of Sai baba, I also received the coveted "National

Integration Award" for the film on 17 July 2002 from the hands of the then President of India, Sh. K.R. Narayanan at Rashtrapati Bhawan, New Delhi.

It is important to believe that Vibhuti is not just a pinch of ash or Bhishma, it is Sanjeevani indeed, just like a lifesaving medicine. Vibhuti is blessed by Sai himself.

It has the power that can turn anything impossible into possible. There are millions of devotees who have personally seen and felt the impact of magical powers of Sai Vibhuti in their lives. Devotees who drink Vibhuti in water, apply it on the neck or forehead with faith and reverence in Sai Baba, get complete relief from sufferings of any kind and get blessed with unexpected benefits. Such is the miraculous glory of Vibhuti!

Alcohol addiction is over

It was the year 2009. There was a truck driver named Paramjit living in Punjab. He was a habitual drinker of alcohol. It was not possible for him to drive without drinking alcohol. He was a complete atheist; he did not believe in any religion at all. He used to tell people that alcohol could not harm him at all because before drinking alcohol, he used to drink a glass of milk.

One day he was sitting in a Roadside hotel (dhaba), watching television. At that time the program "Sai Ki Mahima" was being aired on TV. He watched the program with interest and then, the next day he found out my details to contact me and talk to me. He said, "I have the bad habit of drinking a lot of alcohol. I have been trying hard to get rid of the habit but to no avail. Now I want to give up alcohol permanently. I request you to please send me the Vibhuti that you provide for giving up alcohol. And please also send the cassettes of Sai Baba Bhajans." On his request I dispatched the Vibhuti as well as the Cassettes.

For two months, Paramjeet started taking milk and regularly licking Vibhuti before driving his truck. On the way, he would listen to Baba's songs. This sequence lasted for two months. During this period, he did not consume alcohol even for a single day. Gradually, his life became completely alcohol free. He now consumes Vibhuti instead of alcohol.

One day Sai Baba appeared in his dreams. Baba told him "Now you should start doing farming instead of driving truck. You already have a lot of land in your village. You will be more successful now. And do keep taking Vibhuti every day."

Due to some unknown reason, he vomited blood the very next day. As he became unwell for many days, he could not go on truck driving duty. Even after recovering, he did not wish to go for truck driving and instead started farming in his village. As per Sai baba's directive, he has been doing farming for over ten years. He has also become a staunch devotee of Sai Baba and has been regularly spreading the word about Baba's greatness in areas around his village.

Saved from going for bypass Surgery

This happened in the year 2010. There used to be a lady Ramola Chatterjee who was staying in Chittaranjan Park, Delhi. One day, her husband suddenly had severe chest pain. Ramola got her husband admitted to Batra Hospital. Upon investigation, it was found that his pancreas were very not working and he became weak and critical. As Ramola was associated with Shirdi Sai Baba

Foundation, she telephoned me to discuss. She was much worried and explained everything about her husband's health. I assured her and told her that, "Nothing is going to cause any harm to your husband. He will be saved and will be back to normal soon. Just give him this Vibhuti with water and make him drink it for three to four times a day."

Earlier, after examining, the doctors had said that he would have to undergo bypass surgery in a few days. The woman came back home with her husband. From the very next day, she mixed Vibhuti in water and gave it to her husband and this process was done for a week. After a week, they went to the hospital to get her husband re-examined. Amazingly, her husband's pancreas was fully cured and was functioning normally. The doctors were surprised. With blessings of Sai, now there was no need to go for surgery. This is Vibhuti's magic!

Smallpox scars vanished completely

There was a person named Rohan Chattopadhyay in Maharashtra. His entire body became white due to smallpox. One day, he was watching Sai's glorification program on TV and reached me through my contact resources. He called me and enquired about possibility of its treatment. I asked him to mix Vibhuti in cow dung and apply it on the whole body daily, before taking bath.

Rohan followed the routine as told to him. After a month, all the scars of Smallpox on his body disappeared completely. This is how holy Vibhuti provides solace to Sai baba's devotees.

Pension resumed

This refers to a true incident that took place in year 2009. Meena, who lives in Kerala, belongs to a very simple family. She was associated with the Shirdi Sai Baba Foundation many years ago. She used to love and take care of her parents very much. Her parents were very old and were receiving pension after retirement from a Government job. Suddenly, without any specific reason, their pension was stopped; and big problems started surfacing in their life due to financial crises. Meena had a cow at home and by selling its milk, she was somehow managing things. Unfortunately, soon, the cow expired due to some disease and now, it became extremely difficult for Meena to arrange for food and other essentials. It was not possible for Meena to join a job, leaving behind her ailing parents. She was extremely worried.

Meena had a lot of faith in me and in Sai's Vibhuti. She called me up and explained her problems to me. Immediately, I dispatched Vibhuti for her through speed Post. Meena was delighted having received Vibhuti.

She placed Vibhuti in her Puja room and started worshiping Vibhuti daily with faith and reverence for Sai Baba. In the same month, the pension from the Government department was resumed and their financial problems also ended, bringing back peace and happiness in their lives. The magic of Vibhuti brought back love and laughter in Meena's home.

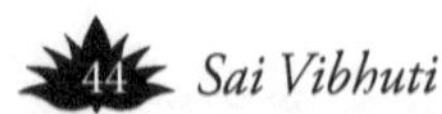

Got freedom from Asthma

A lady named Meenakshi was suffering from Asthma. She had severe joint pain and it was very difficult for her to move from one place to another. She had to use wheel-chair in order to go from one place to another.

Somebody informed me about Meenakshi's upcoming trip to Delhi. I took her contact number and called to inform her that I meet her at the Airport.

I reached the Airport and met Meenakshi. I personally applied Udi on both her knees and also gave her a packet of Udi to take with her. I asked her to apply Udi, mixed with mustard oil, on joints, two times a day. Meenakshi followed my advice and applied Udi on her joints for one month with faith and reverence in Sai Baba's healing powers. Soon, she regained strength in both legs and the pain in joints was also gone. With the blessings of Baba, now she is able to move around without any difficulty and now she also goes for her morning walks regularly. This is how wonderful the Udi is!

Sai's Vibhuti is the biggest troubleshooter.
It represents Sai through its magical powers.
Baba used to give Udi with His own hands to
alleviate the suffering of his devotees.
Even today Vibhuti is doing the same thing.
To know Sai, to believe in Sai,
It is imperative to reach Sai's place.
When you have faith and reverence in your
mind You also have the means
To overcome every crisis.
Holy Vibhuti is bringing peace and prosperity
In the lives of people all over the World.

Got rid of Smoking completely

A person named Praveen used to smoke heavily and it was almost impossible for him to get rid of this habit. He used to spend a lot of money on this bad habit. His financial position was getting bad to worse as whatever he used to earn, was going in smoke. Once, his wife was watching "Sai Ki Mahima" program being telecast on TV. She called up Shirdi Sai Baba Foundation Office and asked for Vibhuti. On receiving Vibhuti, she asked her husband to lick small quantity of Udi. Praveen refused to agree and said, "What sort of medicine is this? Who will consume ash to get cured?"

Her husband was told to talk to me directly so as to understand the procedure and its benefits. I told Praveen, "Whenever you feel an urge to smoke, just close your eyes and put a small quantity of Udi on your tongue. You will soon start feeling better." Praveen agreed to follow my advice and started having Udi whenever he had an urge to smoke. Within 40 days, he was cured from the deadly habit of smoking and never felt the need to smoke. This is how wonderfully Udi brings back happiness and hope in lives of Baba's devotees!

SAI VIBHUTI

'Vibhuti' is the herb for alleviating hundreds of diseases, 'Vibhuti' is the link between God and his Devotee!

'Vibhuti' is a means to get rid of all problems, Oh, 'Vibhuti' is the courtyard of Dwarka Mai!

'Vibhuti' is blessed by Sai, The glory of 'Vibhuti' is spread in the heart of every devotee of Sai.

'Vibhuti' is the priceless gift of endlessly burning Dhooni, Just see, the whole world itself is like 'Vibhuti'.

'Vibhuti' is Holy, Sacred and therapeutic, 'Vibhuti' is filled with the music of Divinity of God.

Writer: Aushim Khetarpal